F

A Co. ͺurary Look at the

Sermon on the Mount

Robert Lee Hamblin

Insight Press
New Orleans

Printed in the United States of America
ISBN 0-914520-32-6

ii

Contents

Introduction

The contents of this book consist of sermons preached by the author. The original purpose was not for publication, but in answer to many request for these sermons in writing, I became convinced that it might be the will of God to share them with a wider audience.

The majority of people today seem to be searching for things that will make them happy. The search for happiness is on everywhere, but usually the results are very disappointing. It has occurred to me that every person in the world would like to be happy. Jesus is the only one that can bring real happiness. When He preached the "Sermon on the Mount," He taught His followers how to be happy. The principles He taught about two thousand years ago still work.

The people who heard the "Sermon on the Mount" were followers of Jesus as their Savior and Lord. No person can ever discover the ultimate of happiness without having faith in Jesus as Savior and Lord. He came to the world to live, die and live again to provide abundant life for all people (Jn.10:10). Real happiness begins with the reception of that eternal life from the Lord.

Upon the reception of the gift of eternal life, believers can obtain happiness in every arena of life if they are willing to live life on God's terms. Many of God's terms for happiness are contained in the "Sermon on the Mount." It would be good for anyone who searches for happiness to study it.

The Lord's sermon began by saying that Jesus saw the multitudes and then went up into the mountain and taught his disciples. He apparently left the multitudes in order to give this discourse to those who had accepted Him. He cared about the hurting multitudes. They were always crowded about Him. He healed them and taught them. Even the Sadducees and Pharisees stopped on occasion to hear Him speak. However they were not ready for these lessons on happiness. Jesus would teach His followers and then send them to the multitudes. The multitudes could not understand or appreciate the things that Jesus would teach. He would get back to the crowds, but first those who knew Him as the Messiah must learn how to be happy in the service of God.

Jesus knew that He was the King of kings and the Lord of lords. He had come to declare His kingdom to the world and to establish His kingdom in the lives of those who would follow Him. He would bring down the walls that separated people by race, culture and class. If that would be done, it must be done by people who believed in Him and who understood the meaning of citizenship in His kingdom. Those who so understood would exude happiness in a world of human failure and need. Jesus came to change the lives of all people who are in His kingdom to the extent that they would joyfully demonstrate God's kingdom ideals. This is what the Master declares in the "Sermon on the Mount."

It is the author's desire that you first make certain that you have a faith in Jesus as your Savior and Lord. Then learn to be a good citizen in God's kingdom. This will lead you into real happiness.

The "Sermon on the Mount" is beautiful in design, style and scope. Jesus preached, as John did, that the kingdom of God was near. In the "Sermon on the Mount," Jesus told His followers what the characteristics of citizens of His kingdom would be. He also spoke of their privileges and duties, all of which would lead to lives that God wanted for them. This was the way to happiness and spiritual success. Jesus established a relationship between His ethical teaching and the teaching of God's moral law. He placed morality on a very high spiritual plane. Jesus does not teach His followers everything they need to know in this sermon, but it is a guide for many things.

Jesus' simple style of presentation was natural and contained vivid and pointed illustrations.

As you study the "Sermon on the Mount," do not try to make it an all inclusive guide for your Christian conduct, but allow its teachings to guide you into good conduct. As a citizen of God's kingdom, you will be able to attain real happiness by following the principles set out by God in the "Sermon on the Mount."

CHAPTER I

HAPPY ATTITUDES

Matthew 5:1-12

Jesus preached "The Sermon on the Mount" from a hill
where He could see a large crowd of people. He taught some
of the most profound things ever taught. "The Sermon on the
Mount" may well be the ultimate statement of the ethical
responsibilities of man. The sermon is a statement of an
ideal Christian code of conduct toward people.

Parts of "The Sermon on the Mount" can be found in Mark,
Luke, and John, but the entire sermon is recorded in Matthew.
There is some debate about the differences in the account of
Matthew and the other writers. It seems that Matthew
recorded the sermon in its entirety. Jesus may have said
even more than Matthew recorded. Other writers used some of
the sayings from the sermon. It is probable that Jesus
taught the same things, using the same words, on several
occasions. Luke recorded the sermon in a shorter form in
Luke 6:20-49. One may account for this shorter version by
understanding that Luke was writing for a Gentile audience,
and he omitted the items that had a strong Jewish appeal.

Matthew, of course, was one of the apostles. He
followed the Lord from the beginning of His ministry. He
recorded the sayings of Jesus that are in "The Sermon on the
Mount." Actually, it is a sermon about the way to happiness.
The subject of the sermon is citizenship in the kingdom of

God. Jesus taught, as John the Baptist did, that the reign of God was near. In this sermon Jesus discussed the spiritual characteristics of those who share in His reign. He connected the conduct of life in His kingdom to the teaching of the law. He was not overturning the teaching of the law, but He gave His followers the spiritual meaning of God's eternal teaching. He showed them how to apply that teaching to their lives, so as to result in a godly contentment and happiness. The sermon has been correctly described as a "point of transition from the law to the gospel."

The sermon is not, as some suppose, to be taken as a summary of all that Jesus taught. He had many other things to say and to do after the sermon was preached. His crucifixion, resurrection, and ascension were before Him. Eternal life would be established for His followers by His death and resurrection. "The Sermon on the Mount" would give His followers some principles of life in relation to other people which would be based on everything that God had done and would do. To take the teaching of Jesus from "The Sermon on the Mount" into one's life brings a meaning to life that can only come from divine understanding. The only way one can truly attain happiness is to understand the teachings of this sermon and to make them a part of one's life.

In this chapter we will study the introduction to "The Sermon on the Mount." This passage is often called the Beatitudes because it is about happiness.

Some people believe that happiness is a frame of mind. They believe that one can create happiness by having a positive attitude. They believe that one can be happy, no matter what happens, if the mind conceives of happiness. This concept does not recognize the existence of evil. When one reads the book of Job, the realization comes that bad things can happen to good people. It takes more than a positive attitude to have real happiness. Happiness comes on God's terms.

God created each person for Himself. Until one comes to God for forgiveness, there is no happy state of mind. In the guilt of sin, there is no true happiness. When Jesus preached "The Sermon on the Mount" He talked to people who knew Him as Savior. His disciples came to Him, and He taught them. A large crowd of people were there, but the Lord left them and spoke to His disciples from the standpoint of their knowledge of Him. From that perspective He taught them how to be happy.

One may be a positive thinker, but evil and sin must be considered. One may be determined to be happy. It may be decided each day that happiness will come in everything that happens. Generally something will happen that is beyond control. How can one be happy in that condition? It is necessary to come to the Lord for forgiveness. He takes evil out of sinful lives, and He is truly able to create happiness. From that perspective the Lord gave the Beatitudes. The Bible says that He saw the crowds and went up on a mountainside where He sat down, and His disciples came and sat down with Him, then He began to teach them.

He had great compassion for the people whom He saw. The Lord still has that great love for His people. He does not want anyone to live a devastated life. He does not want any person to be unhappy and filled with worry. He wants each believer to find peace.

His disciples sat down around Him so they could hear Him teach. They were actually participating in what He was saying. There is a great lesson to be learned in this. When one sits with the Lord and listens, he has fellowship with the Lord. He actually participates in what Jesus is doing in the world. As His disciples participated in the teaching of "The Sermon on the Mount," persons today participate in His work by listening to His Word, believing it and obeying it.

I. Happy Humility (5:3-5)

Jesus began to teach the people saying, "Blessed are the poor in spirit for theirs is the kingdom of heaven." "Blessed (Makarioi)" means happy. Jesus did not begin the sermon with a connecting word or clause, but with the word happy. Surrounded by unhappy, suffering people Jesus talked about happiness. "Happy are the poor in spirit," what a revolutionary concept!

That was different than anything the world had ever heard before. It is different than most of the teachings of today. Today people say that if you want to be successful you must be aggressive. Many people believe that being

4

"number one" is the most important thing in life. At
sporting events people shout, "We're number one!" People
acclaim their own abilities to do all things by their own
power. The Lord taught differently. He taught that He is
number one. Real happiness comes when believers submit to
the Lord. He can bring happiness.

So, Jesus Said, "Happy are the poor in spirit; for
theirs is the kingdom of heaven." Poverty of spirit means
humility and submission. Submission requires trusting God.
This humility does not require that one hang his head all the
time and be sad. It does not mean that one is to be negative
about life. It means just the opposite of that. It means
that the believer understands that the source and power of
life is God. Christians should not depend upon self; they
must depend upon God. This has its reward. Jesus said that
the people who are poor in spirit own the kingdom of heaven.
They are a part of everything that God is doing. God, who
made the world, runs the world. This God who runs the world
is in charge of everything, so everything belongs to Him. If
one trusts God instead of human abilities, God gives His
power to that person. That brings happiness.

Physical wealth alone can not bring happiness. Human
acceptance alone cannot bring happiness. Happiness comes to
those who walk with God. They are the owners of the kingdom
of heaven. They have joy and happiness.

Jesus said, "Blessed are those who mourn for they will
be comforted." Real joy and happiness are greatly

appreciated by those who have known the opposite. In music, the best cords are those that come after discord. The same is true in life. The Lord taught that those who mourn over life's troubles, whether they are physical or spiritual, will be comforted by God. God's comfort is more than equal to the mourning or distress that comes to life.

This Beatitude may be more fully understood by considering that in New Testament times people mourned in a different way than the mourning of Western culture. When someone died in New Testament times, the family hired mourners to wail and make sad sounds. They demonstrated their mourning publicly and openly. That was the way that they expressed compassion. People were hired to mourn and show their compassion for the person who was suffering. The Lord said, "Happy is a person who mourns." He seems to be including the person who has love and compassion for other people.

Some things bring sadness and mourning when they are experienced. Mourning may be triggered in many ways. When a loved one is lost, it brings sadness. That sadness comes because the earthly life is over and this results in separation that brings sadness and tears. However, believers do not sorrow as those who have no hope; because their hope is in the Lord. One cannot know the depths of God's comfort until sadness has been conquered by the promises and the power of the Lord. Jesus taught that having compassion for another person who is living in sorrow brings comfort from

God to both people involved. This makes it possible for people to face the reality of sadness and to have compassion on those who are in sadness. Victory will come from God if Christians trust God for comfort and try to comfort each other. God will intervene, and God will comfort. In times of sorrow, God brings joy and happiness with His comfort. God comes to those who mourn. When He does, He sends His Spirit with the assurance of eternal and abundant life. This brings happiness to the comforted believer.

Jesus said, "Blessed are the meek; for they will inherit the earth." The philosophy of the world is diametrically opposed to this concept. Many people believe that aggression is the way to inherit the earth. God says that happiness comes to the meek, and God Himself will give the earth to the meek. That may seem to be implausible, but God will make it a reality. People really do not own the earth. They may think so, but humans only have an investment in it, not complete ownership. It belongs to God. When people fail to recognize God's ownership, they bring many problems to the environment in which they live.

It is difficult to define meekness. Whether the word is considered in English or Greek, it is hard to define. Meekness includes gentleness and patience. It also indicates freedom from pretension. It implies endurance. Some people think that meekness is being a mild-mannered person who will compromise everything, but meekness seems to mean for the Christian that the life is tamed by the grace of God.

I once knew a man whose business was training rodeo horses. When one of my children was small, we went to visit this man. He had a horse that was wild. No one could get near it. It bucked and jumped around the corral. The horse was mean and wild. A few weeks later while visiting that same family, the man wanted to show me his horse. We went to the corral to find the horse very tame. A bridle and a saddle were on it. He even offered to let my little girl ride the horse. I said, "You're not going to put my little girl on that horse." He assured me that the horse was tame.

God promised that He would bring happiness to the life that is tamed by His grace. The one tamed by the grace of God will inherit the earth. The wildness of sin can only be tamed by the grace of God. People try to remove sin from their lives by good resolutions or desires. They say, "If I could just make up my mind to do it, I could do it." Many are very resolute about quitting their sins, but it never works. The only way to gain control over sin is to submit it to God and let God, by His grace, tame sin. Happiness comes to the meek. Meekness comes through God's grace. The grace of God brings calm and peace to its recipients. They have calm and peace because God is present. They inherit all that God wants to give them.

II. Happy Desires (5:6)

Next Jesus said, "Blessed are those who hunger and
thirst for righteousness." Hunger and thirst are two strong
drives in life. One may do without many things, but not food
and water. The absence of food and water will cause death.
There is something in the human body that makes one know that
food and water are needed. The strongest drives in humans
are the drives for food and drink. God taught that if one
wants to be happy, righteousness must be desired with a drive
as strong as the desire for food and water.

This righteousness is not imputed righteousness. It is
personal righteousness. It is simple goodness. It is doing
what is right in the sight of God. Jesus told His followers
to be perfect. Some retreat immediately from that command
saying, "I cannot be perfect, there is no one perfect but
Jesus." While it is true that Jesus is the only perfect one,
believers are not excused from searching for perfection. How
can that be done? There must be a strong desire for
goodness. Jesus said, "If one has a strong desire for
goodness he will be filled with goodness." This means that
God will forgive sins, and God will give power to believers
enabling them to do what is right.

It is easy to make excuses for one's sins. Many people
like to blame their sins on someone else. Many deny the
reality of sin. If that cannot be done they blame someone
else saying, "It wasn't my fault; it was someone else's
fault." As a last resort some will say, "The devil made me

do it." Each person determines his own desires and the resulting actions; therefore, each person is responsible for his or her actions. One must realize that sin is against God and each person is responsible to God for sin.

The responsibility for sin cannot be removed, but God can change the way His followers act. A follower of Jesus is able to desire goodness. God then will provide that goodness. God does this by providing forgiveness. He cleanses the guilt that is in the believer's life. He takes it away by His own sacrifice. God makes it possible for His followers to have a daily walk with Him. God empowers one to do what is right in His sight. Day by day and moment by moment, one may ask God to fill his life with goodness. The practice of goodness becomes possible by the power of God. God gives the believer the ability to do what is right and this results in happiness.

In the days of Jesus when this sermon was preached, there were people who were not doing right, but they went about bragging how much better they were than other people. They were self-righteous people. There are similar people today. They often condemn everything and everyone. They are so smug that they cause much unhappiness. Self-righteousness is the opposite of the quality of life Jesus wants His followers to have. He wants all believers to desire goodness. This will bring real happiness.

III. Happy Fellowship With God (5:7-12)

Jesus taught His disciples to be merciful. He said, "Happy are the merciful for they will show mercy." This is an important concept for Christians. Jesus taught that believers are to be forgiving and understanding of other people. They must show mercy. Mercy is giving favor where favor is not deserved. God has given His grace and mercy to sinners. If one truly desires happiness, it is necessary to learn to forgive as God forgave. Forgiving is sometimes difficult to do, but God wants His followers to achieve it. Sinful human nature makes it difficult to forgive to the extent that sins are forgotten. That is what God does when He forgives, and that is what He wants from His disciples. Mercy comes from God; therefore, believers should show mercy. By showing mercy, one attains mercy. That mercy comes from God, and from other people.

Next Jesus said, "Blessed are the peacemakers for they shall be called the sons of God." Jesus was a peacemaker. One is doing what God does when he makes peace in the lives of other people. Jesus was called, "the Prince of Peace." When one is a peacemaker, he looks as God looks. He is doing the thing that God does. Therefore, he will be known as the child of God. People sometimes look like their parents. The Bible is saying that one who makes peace does what God does on the earth, and people will identify that person as the child of God. This brings happiness.

Jesus said, "Blessed are the pure in heart." Purity of heart brings happiness. A pure heart is a heart that is set only on God. Jesus said that a pure heart will reveal God. That means that one with a pure heart can be in God's presence now while living on the earth. If one sets his heart on God to live in the power of God and in the ways of God, this will result in fellowship with God now. That brings great joy and happiness. It is a wonderful truth for believers to know that wherever one goes, God goes with him. God is present to give power to do what is right. God commands believers to have a pure heart. To do this one must turn away from sin and turn away from the worldly things that separate him from God. Believers were asked to walk with God in purity of heart. They were promised that this would bring fellowship with God.

Jesus concluded the Beatitudes by telling believers to be happy even when they were persecuted and when they were suffering for the sake of goodness. God's followers have always endured some persecution. Jesus told the disciples that the prophets were persecuted but they depended upon God, and His power was in their lives.

Jesus seems to have become very personal. He seems to have pointed to His disciples and said, "Happy are _you_ when people persecute you and say all manner of evil against you falsely." God must take control of one's life in order for him to have happiness. One must be certain of salvation, then he must submit his life to Jesus as the Lord and Savior.

Life can be filled with many negative things because sin is everywhere. It is impossible to find real happiness without fellowship with God. Fellowship with God can only be attained by submission to God as Master and Lord of our lives.

The Beatitudes teach that happiness comes from God. They also teach that we must recognize our weaknesses and submit ourselves to God. If we do this God will provide real happiness for our lives.

CHAPTER II

HAPPINESS: ATTAINING GOD'S PURPOSE

Matthew 5:13-20

The "Sermon on the Mount," tells people how to live
happy lives. Life is created by God, and human life is made
in God's image. This is a great gift from God. God made
each person free to choose to do good or bad. Being created
in the image of God gives that freedom. God wants His people
to choose good so that they may have fellowship with Him.

When God created Adam and Eve, He put them in a garden
so they could have fellowship with Him. They walked with
Him, and He walked with them in the garden. When they chose
to sin, it separated them from God. Since that time all
people have sinned. Even though we all sin, God wants to
have fellowship with us.

In the "Sermon on the Mount," Jesus talked to His
disciples about accomplishing the purposes of God. When they
attained those purposes, they were happy. In this passage
Jesus talked about the purposes of believers' lives. No
person has the right to live for himself alone. The human
life is created in the image of God and for God. Every
person has a responsibility to God. God created each person
for specific purposes. Sometime one may ask, "Why am I
living?" It is good for one to consider what he is
accomplishing.

The human life is created, by God, for purposes much

greater than animal desires. The acquisition of food, drink, and wealth is not the highest motive. Survival isn't even the best motive. To live in the will and purpose of God is the best motive in life. That motive is the theme of this passage of scripture.

I. The Purpose of Salt

Jesus said, "You are the salt of the earth." It must be remembered that He was talking to His disciples. They believed that He was the Messiah. Because they believed in Him, He called them the salt of the earth. He said, "You are the salt of the earth." Pronouns do not always appear in the Greek, since they are expressed in the verbs. Here, "You," is expressed making it emphatic. Those poor and sometimes despised disciples were, themselves, the salt of the earth. It could be translated, "Even you, are the salt of the earth."

The word are, means that His disciples were already the salt of the earth. It also means that every follower of Jesus since that time has been and is the salt of the earth. People interpret the meaning of salt in several different ways. Some think that it means that those who know the Lord season the earth. They consider salt basically as a seasoning for food. The idea is that Christians can keep life from being tasteless. This is a strained interpretation, and is out of character with the context. Others claim that the salt means that Christians fertilize the lives of others, causing the growth of humanity. That interpretation will not stand in light of the statement that salt can lose its power.

In New Testament times salt was an abundant product, and it was used as a preservative. People were known to bring large quantities of salt into their homes. Since there was no refrigeration in those days, they used salt to preserve food. People in New Testament times would understand that one who is the salt of the earth, is a preservative of the earth. As the salt of the earth, believers preserve the earth.

In Colossians, the Bible stated that the earth is held together by Jesus Christ as Lord of human lives (Col. 1:17). If Jesus could be withdrawn from the earth, it would disintegrate. The world could not exist without the influence of Jesus Christ on human lives.

There is evidence of the destructive power of sin in the world. Human greed has many adverse effects on the environment. Sometimes it seems that the world is disintegrating. It will not disintegrate because Jesus is the Lord of the earth; therefore, the sustainer of the earth. As the Lord of the earth, He gave the quality of salt to believers so that they might become the preservatives of the earth.

Jesus taught that salt could lose its power and no longer be good for its original purpose. When this happens it is thrown out and trodden under the feet of men. Jesus was teaching that the purpose of salt was to preserve.

However, when people brought salt into their homes and left it too long, it lost its power to preserve. When it lost that power, it would be thrown out of the house. The salt would become firm in the rain and sun, and it would make good paths for the people. When salt lost its power it was no longer used to preserve food; it was used for pathways. That was not the original purpose for salt. Its original purpose is to preserve.

The human body has many muscles, if they are not used they become atrophied. The leg muscles make it possible for one to walk or run. However, if a person ceases to use those for a long period, they are weakened and eventually atrophied. The muscles are still there, but they will not do their purpose. God told believers, "You are the salt of the earth." That means that Christians are to use themselves to preserve the earth. If they do not use their lives for this purpose, they will be used for a secondary purpose. When one is saved by the blood of Jesus Christ, he becomes the child of God. God saves people in order that they might live in Him and for Him. They are to have an influence for Him. They are to be witnesses for Him. If one does not use his life as a positive influence for God by witnessing, then the life is used for a different purpose than God had intended.

Many professed Christians apparently are not using their lives as salt. Many churches have inactive members. What is the problem? Many people who call themselves Christians are not using their lives in the way God wants their lives to be

17

used. To fulfill the purpose of God requires believers to read the word of God, listen to God, talk to God and obey the commands of God. They must also give God the glory and the credit for all that He has done in their lives. If those things do not happen, the believer's life will be used for a secondary purpose. No Christian can be happy in that condition. The only way to be happy is to use the life the way that God intends for it to be used. Christians must be the preservatives of the earth if they are to have God's quality of happiness in their lives.

II. The Purpose of Light

Jesus said, "You are the light of the world." Light was very important to the people who heard Jesus speak. They did not have electricity or the brilliant incandescent lights that are seen in modern cities. However, even then, a city located on a hill could not be hidden. At night when they looked over the hills, candles were burning. Fires could also be seen, causing them to know where the city was. Jesus said, "People don't light a candle and put it under a cover so that it is hidden." When one lights a candle he puts it on a candle stand so that it gives light to an entire room. The purpose of a lighted candle is to illuminate the darkness. As the children of God, the disciples were the light of the world. Jesus did not request believers to be light, but informed them that they were light. The children of God are lights in a dark world.

The Bible tells us that Jesus came as light in a world

filled with darkness. "The light was shining in the darkness, and the darkness could not hold back the light" (Jn. 1:4-5). Jesus is still the light that shines in the world. He shines through the illumination given by His followers. He brings light to human lives. He drives out the darkness of guilt, and He gives the light of everlasting life. Because that light is in the believer's life, he must reflect it. Believers illuminate the dark world with the presence of the loving and saving God.

That light must shine in the darkness of the world. If it is hidden, it does not shine. How can it be hidden? How can a Christian put a cover on his light? The light is hidden by those who continue to live in sin. Each time a believer sins, he causes someone to be blinded in darkness, rather than seeing the light. Every Christian has sinned. If one does not want to be a stumbling block, it is necessary to pray and confess sins. This causes the light of God to come into lives and remove sin. Then the light shines in the darkness.

One way believers keep from covering the light is by staying in fellowship with God through confession, and walking with God. A positive attitude about letting the light shine is a necessity. Just as a city on a hill cannot be hidden, Jesus desires for the light of Christian lives to never be hidden. People need to know about God. The only way they can know about the saving power of God is through the light that shines in the lives of believers.

Jesus concluded this matter by saying, "Let your light shine before men, that they may see your good deeds and glorify your Father, which is in heaven." The passage teaches believers to live in such a way that unbelievers may see the light of God in their lives. Seeing this light, they will become believers and attain to the greatest goal of life, which is to glorify God. While the Lord does not teach believers to be ostentatious in the outward expressions of their faith (Matt. 6:1-4), He does teach that the light is to be put in its proper place. Some seem to believe that they should hide their Christian deeds. They believe that is humility. However, there is a time and a place for good works to show and call people to the glory of God.

When I was a very young preacher, I preached in a revival in a rural church. They received a love offering to give me. It was received in small envelopes. At the end of the revival, they did not count the money. They simply gave all the envelopes to me. Many of those envelopes had notes on them, usually a name and an expression of appreciation. However, one had written on it, "Don't let your left hand know what your right hand is doing." I immediately knew that this person was one who thought that all giving should be done privately. That person believed that this was an expression of humility. There, of course, a time for the expression of that kind of humility. There is a time for private communication with God, and for things to be done in private, but there is also a time for things to be done in public. If the light shines correctly, it is not ostentatious, but it glorifies God.

Some people will not come to know God unless they are influenced to come to Him by the testimony or the witness of another person. Jesus said, "Let your light shine before men." The purpose was: "That they may see your good works." Christian works are not to be hidden, but they are to be seen in the open. Certainly, if one does good works only to be seen of men, he is wrong. Jesus taught, later in the "Sermon on the Mount," that believers are not to be hypocrites. He said that hypocrites demonstrated their good works so that people would praise them. While the good works of believers are not to be hidden and are to be seen, it is not for human praise, but to cause others to glorify the Father. Good works are to be done in the name and the power of the heavenly Father. They are not to be done for human glory.

If a believer gives to demonstrate his generosity, he is wrong. That would bring human praise and borders on hypocrisy. If one gives because of love for the Lord, God gets the glory; and it is a good witness. If one preaches because he knows how and has the ability to do it, giving himself the credit, he is not glorifying God. However, if one preaches in the power of God's Spirit, desiring to cause people to glorify God, he is letting his light shine. One must say, "I preach the word of God because God has called me, and because God has given me the grace to do it. God has sent His Holy Spirit into my life to cause me to be able to

do this; therefore, God gets the glory." This is the way
that you let the light shine. If a farmer had an abundant
harvest and he told his friends, "I am a great farmer! I
know how to do it better than anyone else," then he got
credit for himself; his light did not shine. If he says,
"God gave me the seasoning; God smiled upon me and God gave
the increase," then God gets the glory and his light is
shining. If one says, "I have done well in raising my
children; I have used good judgment, and they have turned out
well, so I am pleased with what I have done;" his light is
not shining. If He says, "God has given me the ability to do
it, and God deserves the credit," his light is shining. Let
your light shine. Be the salt of the earth; because this is
the purpose of God.

III. The Purpose of the Law

In the next paragraph, the Lord said that He came to
give a new perspective for life. In that new perspective,
happiness can be discovered. He said, "Do not think that I
am come to abolish the law or the prophets. I have not come
to abolish them, but to fulfill them." The theme of the next
few paragraphs in the "Sermon on the Mount" is taken from
this statement. Jesus was saying, "I did not come to do away
with the law or the prophets, but I came to give them the
meaning that they should have in your life."

The "Sermon on the Mount" is to the New Testament what
the "Ten Commandments" are to the Old Testament. The "Ten
Commandments" gave the people of the Old Testament a theme by

22

which to live. In the "Sermon on the Mount," the Lord is giving the church a theme by which to live. He was saying, "I am not abolishing the theme of the Old Testament, but I am showing what the theme of the Old Testament really means." He said, "I am going to tell you the truth; nothing will disappear, not one jot, not one tittle will disappear from the law until everything is fulfilled in the earth." A jot is a Hebrew letter. That letter is the smallest one in the Hebrew alphabet. A tittle is a very small part of a letter. It is a part of the Hebrew letter "dalleth," which is equivalent to the English letter "D." Jesus was saying that not the smallest letter or the smallest part of a letter will disappear from the law until He gave it its full meaning.

He said, "Anyone who breaks one of the least of the commandments and teaches others to do, the same will be called least in the kingdom of heaven; but whoever practices and teaches these commandments will be called great in the kingdom of heaven." The commandments were to be fulfilled in obedient Christians. The commandments were not only laws written on tablets of stone; they were not simply words on parchment paper; they were words to be etched on human hearts. The law must be fulfilled. It must have its full meaning in the lives of the people who know Jesus Christ. One can read the commandments and conclude that he is guilty of disobedience to God. The purpose of the commandments is to teach people about their guilt. One must accept guilt then submit it to the Lord for His forgiveness. When God has forgiven, He desires that His followers rise above their guilt with all of its negatives. Then one is able to truly be positive about life.

Jesus told the believers not to teach people to break the law. He was telling them to be examples. They were to exemplify goodness in their lives. So, He said, "For I tell you unless your righteousness surpasses that of the Pharisees and the teachers of the law, you will certainly not enter the kingdom of heaven." There were people living in that day who thought that every religious rule was binding upon their hearts. Some claimed that they were living by those rules, actually, knowing that they were not. They were saying, "My theme of life is to keep the commands of God." In their self-righteousness they went about bragging that they were keeping the commands of God while their hearts were evil. They really were not obeying the commands, and they had not committed themselves to the Lord.

If you really want to be happy, your goodness must be better than that. How can your goodness be better? You must submit yourself to the Lord, and let God act out the fulfillment of the law in your life. You must do more than not murder or not commit adultery. You must give yourself to the Lord, so He can give His power to you. If you want to be happy, submit yourself to the Lord of the universe -Jesus Christ. Let Him give you the power over all that is negative and all that is evil.

CHAPTER III

THE FULL MEANING OF THE LAW

Matthew 5:21-26

The only way to find real happiness is to submit
completely to Jesus Christ as Lord. Jesus said that He did
not come to do away with the law, or the ethics of the Old
Testament. He came to give that law its full meaning. Jesus
carefully pointed out to His followers that not one part of
the letter of the law would be abolished. He wanted all
people to understand how to apply the ethical teaching of the
Bible to their lives. One can truly be happy applying those
teachings; because they are eternal instructions. They are
instructions that will work in any society at any time.

Those who break the laws of God are least in the kingdom
of God. They are less than the least in the kingdom of God
if they teach others to break those laws. Jesus taught that
those who practiced the laws of God and fulfilled them in
their lives were great in the kingdom of heaven. He pointed
out that there were religious people in His day, the
Pharisees in particular, who claimed that they believed in
the law; but they did not practice it. They constantly told
people how they were Bible believers, but they did not
practice what the Bible taught.

Jesus carefully pointed out that it was very difficult
for any person to take the letter of the law and do exactly
what it said. He taught that the law had a spiritual meaning

that could not be interpreted by reading the letter of the law. That meaning was understood by developing the right attitude toward other people.

Jesus began this instruction concerning the fulfillment of the law by showing people how to have happy relationships to other people.

I. Regarding Relationships

In light of the fact that all people are created in the image of God, it is strange that it is difficult for people to have good relationships with other people. All people are created in the image of God. Though that is true, often people find barriers between themselves and others. Instead of trying to resolve those barriers many people develop more barriers. Some people do not accept others because they are different. One can never be happy as long as that kind of attitude exists. Some people consider others as enemies, without even knowing them. Some are considered enemies because they live in a different culture. One cannot be totally happy with that attitude. The Lord taught that believers must rise above that kind of thinking.

Jesus said, "You have heard that it was said of the people long ago, do not murder, and any one that murders will be subject to judgment." That was the teaching of the law, and Jesus believed that it was true. God did command people not to murder. One should not take another human life. Human life is a gift from God. One has no right to take the life of another person. That command has stood through the ages. Most of the people who have lived have respected that command. There are people who do not respect it. They usually go to prison, or lose their own lives.

God taught that happiness requires much more than the abstinence from murder. God wants His followers to have control of their attitudes toward other people. He said, "But I tell you that anyone who is angry with his brother will be subject to judgment." Remember that the Lord was teaching people how to fulfill the law in their lives. The law said, "You are not to kill," but Jesus said that the way you fulfill that is not to be angry with your brother.

Can one control anger? I certainly think so. I have seen it done. I had a relative who had a bad temper. He was known for his temper. He would get mad at most anything and display his wrath. When he got mad, he always explained it by saying, "Oh, well, I inherited that." He would conclude by saying that he could not help it. However, I observed that relative very closely. I watched when he got angry and when he didn't get angry. I noticed that when certain people were around, like the preacher, or someone that he wanted to impress, he never did get angry. That taught me that this relative, who even bragged about his bad temper, could control it.

Anger can get out of control. It is something that causes people to do things that they would not normally do. It can cause sin in one's life. The Lord said, "If you really want to be happy, don't be angry at anyone." Anger should be controlled. There are certain things that should arouse indignation in Christians. The Lord Himself became indignant at the people blaspheming the temple of God. He drove them out of the temple. Apparently, He was angry, but He had a controlled anger. His actions were done in divine righteousness.

While it is true that Christians must take a stand against things that are wrong they should never let the emotion of anger take control of their lives. If one does that, he will say and do the wrong things. This usually results in verbal or physical violence toward another person. That action would necessitate an apology.

Jesus taught that happiness requires control of anger. He said, "You will be subject to judgement if you do not control your anger." He was talking about the judgement of God. God is concerned about the relationships people have with each other. He is also concerned about the relationships people have with Him. One must have forgiveness of sins in order that he might have a good relationship with God. God is also concerned about our relationship to each other. The human relationship to God is a vertical relationship. That vertical relationship influences all horizontal relationships. If one desires to control anger, God must be in control of that life. If you find yourself becoming angry at another person stop and say, "Lord give me strength and be my victory over this." Ask God to remove your anger. God will give you the victory over your anger.

Jesus said, "Do not say to your brother, <u>Raca</u>." The word "<u>Raca</u>" is an Aramaic word that was used in the New Testament. The word means , "blockhead." Jesus was teaching us not to think of other persons as ignorant. A blockhead was one who did not know anything. Usually persons who call other persons ignorant are trying to elevate themselves. They are trying to do this at another person's expense. One cannot be happy in that state. The world is competitive. Most people of the world do not serve God. Many are attempting to step over other people to get where they want. When they get to that place they are still not happy. They are trying to succeed, but when that is done at the expense of others it does not bring happiness. Happiness comes to believers who respect others.

Jesus spoke in very practical terms. He said, "If one calls a person a blockhead then that person may take his assailant to court." The Sanhedrin was the Supreme Court of the Jews. One could be brought to the Sanhedrin for calling another "blockhead." It is true today that if one does not have the proper attitude toward others, he will be unhappy. This bad attitude robs one of peace and results in trouble. God taught that believers should not allow this to happen to them. Believers need to respond positively to other people, even in adversity. Some people are evil and they do evil things. They must be left in the hands of God. One must remember that every person is created by God. Each person has the same rights under God. Each one has the same privileges. This brings varying ideas and culture. Rather than judge each other, Christians are to respect all other people. If a person has a different perspective than you, do not consider that person as worthless or useless; that robs the human life of happiness.

Jesus took this another step. He said, "But anyone who says, you fool, will be in danger of hell fire." He had already taught believers to control their anger. If one is angry at others, he will do the wrong things. He will hurt himself. Jesus taught that one should never call another a blockhead; meaning an unintelligent, useless person. That results in human judgement. If one calls another a fool, it results in God's judgement.

The word fool was used by the people in Jesus's day to refer to a person who had absolutely no value. If a person was called a fool, he was being considered as less than human. If one comes to the place in life where he can look on another person as less than human; thus, losing all respect for that person as the creation of God, then it indicates that his own relationship with God is wrong. A person who calls another a fool needs to make sure of his salvation, because he is in danger of going to hell. When one is saved by the blood of Jesus Christ, he is born again. He has a new life, and it is a life of love. If one loves God and is saved by Jesus Christ, he loves the people who are created by God. He shows that love by caring about others.

That would make it impossible for one to have the kind of attitude which calls another person worthless. That kind of dehumanizing attitude is held by many. That attitude brings war. It is the source of bigotry and hatred. One cannot be happy when he centers all of life around himself.

Some arrogant people seem to be happy. Usually, those people are inwardly miserable. Ultimately arrogance brings ruin to the human life. If one can look on other people as of no account under God and in the human race, then his own relationship with God is wrong.

The word "fool" is a very strong word. It is used in a different way in our language than it was in the ancient Aramaic. We refer to a person as foolish and think that it is good. We think that they are jesters or someone who entertains us. That was not what God was talking about. He was talking about the value that one places on another human life. If a person could look on another human being as being unimportant to society, or he can consider that person as one who is unimportant to God; then his heart is not right with God.

II. Regarding Worship

It was very important to Jesus that believers properly relate to other people. He said, "Therefore, if you are offering your gift at the altar and there remember that your brother has something against you, leave your gift there in front of the altar; first go and be reconciled to your brother and come and offer your gift."

What does it take to make one happy? Certainly it makes people happy to worship God. It makes believers happy to be in the house of the Lord. Happiness comes when people read the word of God and hear from the Lord. It makes people happy to pray. However, God taught that one's ability to worship is affected by his attitudes and his relationships to other people. The people who first heard the "Sermon on the Mount" worshiped in the temple. A part of their worship was expressed by bringing sacrifices to the altar of God. These sacrifices brought forgiveness of sins, so they were very important. Christians worship by going to church and praising the Lord who has given them salvation. That is important to Christians. Jesus said, "If you are ready to worship me, and you remember that your relationship with another person is not right; then you must go to that person and settle that relationship." You cannot be happy, even in worship, unless the problem is solved.

Jesus taught that our relationships to other people are more important than our worship. If those relationships are not good, worship is ineffective. People respond to worship in different ways. Some who have been with the Lord, praise Him. Some never worship while in His house. Some act as though they don't care. They act out of duty, and they are glad when worship is over. Why do some sincerely worship and others do not? The difference is within the worshipers. If one walks with God and submits himself to God, worship becomes a great experience. God leads the worshiper to have the right attitude toward other people. If worship is not a great experience, it may indicate that the worshiper needs to get things right with other people. The Lord taught Christians to settle controversies immediately. If there is anything wrong between a Christian and another person, it should be settled immediately. Perhaps one says, "The difficulty is not my fault." Regardless of fault, It is important for believers to turn to the Lord for strength to do what needs to be done to have peace with other people.

One's entire fellowship with God is related to this matter. If happiness is to exist, these matters must be settled. Jesus said, "Settle matters quickly with your adversary who is taking you to court." He taught His followers to settle these matters without going to court. He said, "While you are walking down the road with them, talk it out and get it settled so that you have the right relationship." Jesus said, "If you don't do that, you may end up paying a fine or you may end up in prison."

In summary, the Lord taught His followers that the law taught them not to commit murder. All believers know that they should not take another human life. Jesus taught that real happiness requires much more than obedience to that command. To be happy, all bad attitudes toward other people need to be eliminated. Even worship is ineffective when one harbors bad attitudes toward others. One must be sure of his love for God. If one has love for God flowing through his life, it extends to other people. This eliminates murder, and it also creates a loving attitude that God can use in His kingdom. To do this requires that one walk and talk with God. If you have a problem in your life in relationships toward other people take it to the Lord in prayer. Ask God to forgive you and give you the right attitude toward other people. Ineffective worship may be caused by these bad attitudes. Get things right with other people so that you may freely worship God. This will bring happiness.

CHAPTER IV
HAPPY RELATIONSHIPS
Matthew 5:27-48

The past two chapters have been about the fulfillment of the law of God in human lives. God's law given in the Old Testament taught people how to live. It also taught people about their failures.

Jesus said that He came to fulfill the law. He came to teach people how to be happy by giving the full meaning of the law to people who follow Him. In the last chapter we discussed attitudes that cause happiness. In this chapter Jesus tells us about proper relationships to the opposite sex. He also tells us about honesty and dishonesty. Then He talked about retribution in the lives of believers.

Jesus said to the people of the first century, "You have heard it said that you shall not commit adultery." That command still stands. It is for all people, especially for those who know Jesus Christ. Jesus desired His followers to have higher ethical standards than those of the people who do not know Him. He wanted people to control their actions. When actions were out of control, He wanted His followers to know how to deal with that.

I. The Right Attitude Toward the Opposite Sex

The correct attitude about sexual relationships needs to be observed very closely. People need to hear from God in this matter today. Many attitudes held in today's world are different than the implicit teaching of God in the matter of sexual relationships.

I once knew a very godly man who walked with the Lord. He said to a group that he had absolutely no difficulty in sexual temptation. He believed that he would never sin against God in this manner. However, that same man fell into temptation and the guilt of sin in a sexual relationship.

The Lord taught people how to deal with this. One must do more than make resolutions about adultery. It is necessary for believers to get in control of their attitudes. Jesus said, "If a man looks upon a woman to lust after her, he has already committed adultery in his heart." Jesus taught His followers not to get in situations where they could be tempted to commit adultery. One should not look at pornography or anything that might cause sexual temptation. Christians should turn from that. Looking can result in sin. Some of the strongest drives in human lives are sexual drives. Satan can use those drives to cause the very best people to fall in sin. David fell into this sin. Many others, sometimes even godly people, have fallen in this sin.

In there an answer? Yes! Believers must submit to the Lord and allow Him to be in control. The believer needs to get free from any sexual temptation. When temptation comes, the Christian must turn quickly to the Lord.

Jesus dealt with those who had committed adultery. He said, "It is better for you to cut off your right hand or pluck out your eye than to perish in hell." There were people in His presence who had committed the sin of adultery. He taught them to quit doing that. Did He literally mean for them to cut off their hands and to pluck out their eyes? He was not teaching them to mutilate their bodies. He was saying, "Get your hand and your eye under control." If one could not control his hands and eyes, he would be better without them.

If one looks lustfully, he must repent and confess it. One does not literally pull out his eye, but he does not continue to look lustfully. He must come to God and turn his temptation over to God, then God forgives. Jesus wanted believers to get their entire bodies under control by repenting and confessing sins. If one repents and confesses, he does not continue to do the sin. He ceases from the sin. That is how the eyes and the hands are controlled.

The Lord taught in this passage that happiness comes to those who control their sexual desires by allowing God to be in control of their lives. He was also saying that those who have committed adultery should confess it to the Lord, and repent of it, then they should cease from doing it.

Jesus said, "It has been said that anyone who divorces his wife should give her a certificate of divorcement." That is the same teaching that is in the law recorded in Deuteronomy. In the early years of Israel there were men who would get tired of their wives and make them leave. God did not want that. For the protection of women, He said in His law that women must be given a writing of divorce. This allowed them to be free. Jesus did not allow divorce for any just cause. He taught that when a partner in a marriage commits adultery, that partner has broken the marriage. In that circumstance divorce is permitted by the Lord.

There were differing attitudes about divorce in New Testament times. Some of the teachers believed that divorces could be granted for almost any offense. Jesus did not agree with that. He believed that the one reason for a divorce was if one of the marriage partners committed adultery. Jesus was well acquainted with the scriptures. He knew that the command in the law to give a woman a writing of divorce was for the protection of women who were being mistreated (Deut. 24:1-5). He was also acquainted with the fact that God hates divorce (Mal. 2:16). Jesus believed in the sanctity of the home. He wanted husbands and wives to stay together for their entire lives. This is not a proof-text for divorce. It is a text that teaches married people not to commit adultery. Jesus was granting that divorce is permissible when adultery is committed, but He taught that believers should not commit adultery.

Jesus taught that believers should protect the sanctity of their homes. The Christian home is to be protected at any cost. True happiness can never be attained without happy home life. Adultery cannot bring happiness. Therefore, all lust must be submitted to the Lord for His power to bring victory.

What is to be done by a person who has committed

38

adultery? That person must repent and confess the sin to God. Then Christians must get the matter right with one another. The believer must have a Christian marriage and a Christian home. This is the way to be happy. True happiness is not found in the ways of sin and worldliness; it is found in obedience to God. The book of Proverbs says much about this. It teaches that the way of sin is inviting but it has a bitter consequence. If one wants the sweetness and beauty of life, he must walk with God. Attitudes must be controlled by the power of God if real happiness is attained.

II. Ethical Standard for Happiness

In the next paragraph of the scripture, the Lord taught that honesty is necessary for happiness. Being honest is a part of having the right attitude toward other people. Only with that right attitude can a person be happy. Jesus said, "You have heard that it was said to the people long ago, 'do not break your oath but keep your oaths you made to the Lord.'" Here Jesus quoted the law as it was taught in the Old Testament, but He talked about the law as it was being interpreted by teachers in His time. There were teachers in the New Testament era, who worked out an elaborate system of swearing. There were certain things by which they could swear, and they had to tell the truth. There were other things by which one could swear and he did not have to tell the truth. The interesting thing is that only certain people knew the things that were binding; therefore, they could lie anytime they wanted too. Sometimes I think that we still have a system like that. Jesus completely separated Himself from dishonesty. He said, "There is nothing by which one can swear. One cannot swear by Jerusalem because it belongs to God." Jesus was saying that all things belong to God. No one has anything by which he can swear. "One cannot swear by his hair; because he cannot make one hair white or black." It is interesting that the Lord said this. People try to change hair color. Some who have gray hair, try to make it black. One may color the outside of the hair, but that is all he is able to do. The color may even saturate through the pigment of the hair, but when it grows out from the scalp, it is still white. The Lord taught that people do not own the hair on their heads, so they cannot swear by it. The crux of the matter is this: one does not need any system of swearing if he has the right attitude toward other people.

Jesus said, "Let your 'yes' be a 'yes' and your 'no' be a 'no'." The Lord simply taught that Christians should tell the truth. Life would be wonderful if everyone told the truth. Sometimes it would be embarrassing, but the benefits would far outweigh the problems. God is very sincerely and honestly teaching Christians to tell the truth. When you say "yes," let it be "yes." When you say "no," let it be "no."

I remember that one of the very important things to my father was to tell the truth. He said, "My word is my bond." He did not find it necessary to sign papers when he made deals with his friends. They shook hands because their word was bond. It ought to be that way with all of us. Our

"yes," should be a "yes," and our "no," should be a "no."
Business and society would be better if people would do what
the Lord taught in this matter. One does not need a law to
tell when truth is necessary. If honesty prevailed, the
political and social structures of society could be radically
altered.

The next paragraph teaches some of the most important
ethical concepts in the word of God. Jesus said, "You have
heard that it has been said, 'an eye for an eye, and a tooth
for a tooth,' but I tell you do not resist an evil person.
If someone strikes you on the right cheek, turn to him the
other also, and if someone wants to sue you and take your
tunic, let him have your cloak as well. If someone forces
you to go one mile, go with him two. Give to him who asks
you, and do not turn away from the one who would borrow from
you."

Jesus taught four things in this passage. First He
said, "You have heard that it was said, an eye for an eye,
and a tooth for a tooth.'" That was the way the law was
being interpreted in the days of Jesus. Uncontrolled passion
says, "An eye for an eye and a tooth for a tooth." It is
human nature to hit a person who has struck you. Tiny
children do this as well as adults. That reaction comes
from sinful impulses. Adults seem to think that you can
correct all wrong by fighting the evil doer. Many people
think that it is the way it should be. According to many
people in today's world that is the only way to live. Jesus

said that the opposite is true. He said, "If someone strikes you on the right cheek, turn the other cheek." That is very difficult to do. The only way that can be done is by the power of God. When someone hits another person the immediate physical and emotional reaction is to strike back. Jesus said, "Turn the other cheek." Some try to be funny in interpreting this passage. They tell about some meek preacher who turned the other cheek and then got up after he was struck down the second time and said, "That is all the law requires." Then he fought back. That is neither humorous nor correct.

Simon Peter, a man very much like us, asked the Lord how many times he should forgive in one day. Simon thought seven times would be generous. Jesus Said, "Seventy times seven" (Matt. 18:21). That is four hundred and ninety times. Jesus actually taught believers to forgive as much as is necessary. That may not seem practical; however, Jesus, who is the Lord of life taught this truth. It is practical when the entire scope of life is considered. If one wants to find ultimate happiness, it is necessary to turn the other cheek. This will bring victory in human relationships.

Jesus illustrated the truth of this matter with two possible experiences. He said, "If someone sues you to take away your overcoat, give your suit coat also." The next illustration explains this. He said, "If someone compels you to go a mile, go with him two miles."

The people who first heard this teaching had been

conquered by the Roman armies. The hated Roman soldiers were everywhere about them. The Romans had a law allowing a soldier to compel a subject to carry his pack for one mile. A Roman soldier could approach one of the Jewish people and throw his one hundred and twenty pound pack at his feet. He could say, "You pick it up and carry it for a mile." The conquered person had to do it. Jesus taught believers to carry the pack for one mile; and then when they came to the end of the first mile, they were to tell the soldier, "I carried it one mile because of the law, but I am going to carry it another mile because I want to." Who is master of the second mile?

Saved people do some things beyond the compulsion of duty. Some things are done because of love for God. The world and the people of the world can be very compelling. Believers must always act out of love for God and for people as the creatures of God. This causes believers to go the second mile. The second mile is always a journey of victory.

The natural impulse of most people is to strike back when they are accosted. However, victory and happiness are in the hands of the Lord. How can one find strength to turn the other cheek and to go the second mile? This is done by submission to Jesus Christ as Lord. It is not done by human reasoning, physical force, or human power. It is not done because it is supposed to be done. One must let God take control of His life. God's power brings victory. Can one go the second mile? The natural impulse would be to throw the

43

pack of the Roman soldier down in the dirt and kick dust on it. However, God's power comes to those who show love when they have been despised. The Holy Spirit makes that demonstration of God's love a real possibility. Yes, one can go the second mile in ethical matters.

Jesus summarized the attitude of happiness. He said, "You have heard that it was said love your neighbor and hate your enemies. I tell you love your enemies and pray for those who persecute you that you may be the sons of your Father in heaven." He said that God treats everyone the same way. He causes the sun to come up on the good and the bad. He causes the rain to fall on the good and the bad. This means that Christians should treat everyone with love. They are not to love just one person. Some people are easy to love and some are difficult to love. Believers are to love both groups and exclude hatred. Jesus taught that believers were acting as the children of God when they prayed for the people who persecuted them. Jesus Christ Himself prayed for those who crucified Him. He wants all believers to love even their enemies and to pray for them. When a believer does this he is acting in the character of God.

Jesus said, "If you love those who love you, what are you doing more than others." This is one of the most significant questions in the Bible. Ask this question of yourself. "Because I am saved by Jesus Christ and I know Jesus Christ as my Savior and Lord, what am I doing more than other people are doing?"

Jesus said, "If you greet the ones who greet you, anyone can do that." He said, "If you like the people who like you, anyone can do that." It is easy to respond in kindness to those who are kind. It is difficult to respond kindly to those who are mean. However, the children of God can return kindness to those who are mean to them. Believers can do more than others because they are the children of God.

There are attractive people who are easy to love. There are people who do nice things who are easy to love. There are unattractive people who do bad things. They are not easy to love. As the child of God, you have the power to love them.

Jesus concluded this by saying, "Be perfect as your heavenly Father is perfect." People conclude that they cannot be perfect. Jesus Christ is perfect. He is the pattern of perfection. All humans are imperfect. However, no one has committed a necessary sin. All have committed many sins, but not one person has ever committed a necessary sin. Believers should move toward the completed life that God wants them to have. Most people believe that since perfection seems to be impossible, there is no need to consider it. They consider the command to be perfect irrelevant. It is a relevant command from the Lord. The word translated perfect from the Greek (teleio), meant to be complete. God understands our sinfulness. He has provided forgiveness for our sins. He wants each believer to strive every day for completion. The way to strive for perfection or completion is to submit the human life to God. God makes it possible for His followers to do what is right. He makes perfection possible from His divine perspective. Happiness grows as the believer strives for completion.

Happiness comes to those who allow the law to be fulfilled in their lives. One must not commit murder. Obedience to God is possible for Christians; because they have learned to control their attitudes toward people. One can keep from committing adultery; because he has learned to submit himself to God. One can abstain from divorce by creating a happy home in the power of Christ. Believers are to be truthful by letting God control their words. Christians have the power to turn the other cheek and go the extra mile because they know the Lord. They do not despise their enemies, but they love people through the power of God by submitting themselves to the God who cares. Believers ought to be growing spiritually every day. One should not be satisfied until complete spiritual maturity is attained. This is the journey to happiness.

CHAPTER V

HAPPINESS THROUGH GIVING AND PRAYING

Matthew 6:1-15

In the sixth chapter of Matthew Jesus talked about three elements of worship: giving, praying and fasting. In this study we will look at the first two of those elements of worship.

Jesus began by cautioning believers. They were to be careful not to act as unbelievers acted. They were to be careful that they did not give their offerings as the people gave who did not know the Lord. He told them to be careful that they did not pray as those who did not know God. Believers must never be hypocritical in their worship of God. A happy life requires a right relationship with God. One must stay in fellowship with God and have the proper kind of fellowship with God.

Jesus said, "Be careful not to do your acts of righteousness before men to be seen of them, if you do this you will have no reward from your Father." Jesus used the word "hypocrite." This word is an ugly word to most people. People do not want to be called "hypocrites." The word hypocrite comes from the Greek language. It means to act a part that is not real. A stage actor, in the Greek culture, was a hypocrite. The Lord was saying, "Do not act out your religion, but let your religion be real."

I. Giving

First, Jesus talked about giving. One of the common practices in the days of Jesus was giving alms, or giving to the poor. Some of the people apparently were very hypocritical about their alms giving. They did it for political reasons. They gave in order that someone might see them give, or hear that they gave, and think well of them for their public generosity. Jesus said, "Be careful not to do your acts of righteousness before men to be seen of them." That is the wrong motivation. Any religious act is to be done for the Lord and not to be done to make one popular with the people. Jesus taught that the public display of giving robbed the believer of the heavenly rewards of giving. He warned that motives as well as deeds are important to God. The individual who gives knows his motives as well as his deeds. The rest of the world cannot know his motives. They can only know his deeds. One must be careful that his motives are right.

Jesus said, "When you give to the needy, do not announce it with trumpets as the hypocrites do in the synagogues and on the streets to be honored of man." Evidently there were people in New Testament times who wanted to be honored by men; so when they did their alms giving, they did it in public places. They did it in the synagogue where there was a great crowd, or they did it on the street corners where they could be seen by many people. Some, apparently, even hired trumpeters in order that they might attract a crowd to see their giving. Their motives were wrong. They gave to the poor to be seen of men. They were hypocrites.

Those who did this did not have any reward from God. They already have their reward; they wanted to be seen by men; they were seen. They got what they wanted and there is no other reward.

Jesus turned to the positive aspects of giving. He said, "When you give to the needy, do not let your left hand know what your right hand is doing, so that your giving may be in secret. When your Father sees what is done in secret, He will reward you." Christians are to be sure that they have the right motive when giving gifts in the name of God. One should never give for public display. Giving is not for self-satisfaction. That is the meaning of God's word which teaches that one should not let one hand know what the other hand is doing. One does not serve for self-satisfaction, but believers must please God when they give. When one gives because of love for God, the heavenly Father sees the gift and rewards the gift. Some believe that this means that Christians will get back from God everything they give. God did not promise a large bounty for givers, but He did promise to take care of all needs. From God's prospective of sovereign grace, He promises His blessing to those who honor Him. His reward is not a pay back on an investment. God promises to bless His followers if they honor and serve Him because of simple love.

Service to God that is properly motivated brings great happiness. The proper motivation is love for God. Benevolent giving must be motivated by love for God. If one serves God as a public display to please people, he misses the great reward that God gives, and he misses the happiness that God gives.

II. Praying

The Lord discussed a second element of worship which is praying. He said, "And when you pray do not be like the hypocrites for they love to pray standing in the synagogues and on the street corners, to be seen of men. I tell you the truth, they have received their reward."

There were certain people in the days of Jesus who enjoyed praying in public places. They wanted people to hear them and say, "Oh, what a religious man this is; what a beautiful prayer he is able to pray." Jesus said their motivation was to be heard of men. They were heard, so they have already received all the reward they will receive. That kind of action is not real prayer. God does not hear it. God does not answer it. If the person praying tries to impress other people, his reward is that he is seen by people. He is not rewarded with answer to prayer.

The principle involved in this can be applied to any act of religious service. If motivation in religious service is to be seen by people in order that they might think that the Christian is wonderful, then there is no blessing from God. Believers want God to hear their prayers. They are prayed as communication from person to person. When God hears, He answers.

Jesus said, "But when you pray, go into your room, close the door and pray to your Father who is unseen, then your Father who sees what is done in secret will reward you." Believers are to have conversations with God when they pray. Prayer is not a conversation with other people, but it is a conversation with God. When God said, "Go into your room, or go into your closet," He taught believers to get into the presence of God. They were then to close out all of the elements of the world and be in God's presence.

Not very long ago a man told me that he did his best praying while he was out on a lake in a boat. He said, "I am surrounded by the nature of God, and I do my best praying there." I answered him, "I do my best praying when I get in a place where I am not even aware of nature, or the people around me, or even of my surroundings. I am only aware of the presence of God." I think that is the teaching of this passage of scripture. Jesus taught people to get into the presence of God where all the elements of the world are set aside. You do not need to literally get in the closet, but you must meet God. Jesus taught people to get into the presence of God for prayer. In God's presence they are to talk to the Lord and tell Him what is on their hearts. The heavenly Father will hear and reward openly. This means that God will answer prayers. I really believe in my heart that every prayer we pray to the heavenly Father, in sincerity, in

51

the name of the Lord Jesus Christ, God will answer. He may not give you what you asked for; because you may not need it. Some pray for things out of lust, as James said. Some ask outside of the will of the Father. However, if one is tuned to the will of the Father and is really talking to Him, He answers prayer in the proper way.

Jesus taught believers that they should not pray as the pagans do. They only offered formal prayers. They thought that they were heard for the kind of language that they used in their prayers. Some thought they were heard because they had long prayers. They repeated certain things in their prayers to get the attention of their idols.

Our God is alive. He created each person in His own image. The human spirit, through Christ, can be tuned to the heavenly Father. When that occurs, one can simply tell God what he wants. Christian prayers are conversations with God. Would it not be absurd if you were going to have a conversation with me, and you would write out a formal presentation and repeat it six or eight times. It would be strange if you would use a language that I do not understand in a conversation. I would not want you to talk to me like that. I would want us to sit down together and you tell me what you want to say to me and let me respond. This is exactly what God is saying about prayer. He is saying, "You tell me what you have on your heart, and I will answer you, because I already know what you need." Does that mean that we should not take our needs to God? No, we must take our needs to God. We take them, understanding that He loves us and He knows what our needs are. Therefore, we can take every need to this loving God.

Conversation means that two people talk. Prayer is two or more conversing. When God says, "I know your needs, and I will answer," He is saying that He will talk to us in prayer. Can one truly hear God talk? Yes, God talks. He does not speak in a voice. God speaks person to person without using symbols such as a voice. A voice is something that God placed in humans. People use the vocal cords to make certain sounds that will be intelligible to other persons. Those sounds fall on the ears and send messages to the brain. God does not use vocal cords and ears. He speaks person to person. One really talks to God in the Spirit of the Lord Jesus Christ, then God answers. A voice will not be heard. If God wanted to speak in a voice, He could. He did with Paul, but that is not ordinarily the way He talks. Usually, God speaks to human minds and spirits. God causes people to understand that He is present and that He is answering prayer.

In the rest of this passage, Jesus gave an outline for prayer. It is a very wonderful outline that teaches people how to pray. People often call this the Lord's prayer. Actually, it is a model prayer. It is the outline for praying. Jesus would not have prayed the elements in this prayer. For example, He had no need to ask for forgiveness, but He knew that each believer would have need to ask for forgiveness, so He taught people how to pray for forgiveness.

He said, "Our Father in heaven, Hallowed be Thou name." The first element of real Christian praying is to address God as Father. This requires recognition that God owns all things and He is the Lord of all things. That means that all people are responsible to Him.

When people say, "Our Father," they are saying, "God is the One who made us, and we are responsible to God. God is also the one who owns me; He is the Lord of my life." There is recognition that God is the source of all things, and that means that people are totally dependent on Him. He is the Father in heaven. This means that His Lordship over the universe must be acknowledged. He is not only the Father of those who know Him through Jesus Christ, but He is the Father of all things. The world was made by Him and it is held together by Him. He is the Father who is in heaven; and, therefore, who is in charge of all things.

Prayer is addressed to Him as the Holy Father. His name is to be reverenced. He is not another human being. People are created in His image and their spiritual existence is like His spiritual existence. The Father does not allow human familiarity. He is a Holy God, and in that sense, He is above us. He is other than we are. He is perfect. There is no sin in His life. Though people believe in Christ, they are still sinners. They have wrong in their lives, so every sinner must come humbly before the Father. They come worshipping the name of the Father.

I have friends who think that the only way to pray is on one's knees. I respect that; because that is an act of reverence on their part. I know some who think that the only way to pray is on their faces. I know some who think the way to pray is to stand. I know some who say the only real praying is done in silence. Some think that the best praying is done in public or with other people. The real truth of this matter is the position of the physical body is not the important thing. Whether you are with someone or by yourself is not important. The real thing of importance is that you reverence the name of God to whom you pray. If you can do that better on your knees, then be on your knees. If you can do that better on your face, then do it on your face. Make sure that you reverence the name of the Father. Some people call God, "The Man upstairs, or The Great He." He doesn't want to be addressed in that manner; He wants to be reverenced. When Christians pray, they go to Him in the name of our Lord Jesus Christ and reverence the very name of the Father.

The second thing that Jesus said in this outline on prayer is: "Your kingdom come; Your will be done, on earth as it is in heaven." When Jesus says, "Your kingdom come," He was saying that He wanted God's work to be accomplished in this world. God made the world as a place for people to live. The whole world belongs to Him. This world is the environment made by God for people created in His image. God desires for this world to be exactly the way He made it. He created it in perfection, then people sinned and made it imperfect. They continued to sin, and people are still making it less perfect day by day. God taught people to pray that the kingdom of heaven will come to the earth. This means that each individual is to pray for the will of God to be done on earth as it is in heaven. Sometimes when I pray, the only way I know how to pray is to ask God what His will is; then when I have a revelation of God's will, I know how to pray in the will of God. Believers need to make sure that their prayers are in the will of God.

Jesus said, "Give us this day our daily bread." God wants Christians to ask for their needs in life. God is so wonderful that He is concerned with the daily needs of all humans. He gives daily bread. People need many things. They need places to live, water to drink, and clothes to wear. God is interested in every human need. Each personal need that one has can be brought to God. He did not invite the extravagance of humanity to be brought to Him. He would turn down our request made for extravagant things, but He does invite the real needs of humanity to be brought to Him. Emotional and physical needs as well as spiritual needs will be met by those who pray and trust Him.

Jesus said, "Forgive us our debts, as we also have forgiven our debtors." People are to pray for forgiveness. Most praying people do ask God for forgiveness. People feel a great need in their lives for fellowship with God. The only way that people can have fellowship with God is to have

forgiveness from God. God taught people to ask Him for
forgiveness. There is a limitation in this element of
prayer. Believers must pray that God will forgive them as
they are willing to forgive others. It is easy to be harsh
in criticism of other people. The Lord wants people to be
forgiving. They are to exercise the spirit of love which God
has given after asking God for forgiveness. All believers
need forgiveness every day. That need must be brought to the
Lord in prayer. One must trust God to forgive. Forgiveness
is to be accepted from God, then the forgiven believer must
be forgiving.

Jesus said in His prayer, "Lead us not into temptation,
but deliver us from evil." God is the only one who has power
over evil. When people are tempted they want to say, "Satan
made us do these things." Never does Satan make a Christian
do anything. He places the temptation before believers, but
God has power over Satan. If the believer submits to the
Lord, then God gives victory over evil. God delivers His
children from evil. Evil is a very serious matter.
Christians need the power of God at all times. They need to
pray, "Lord deliver us from the evil one." Humans can't
deliver themselves from the evil one, but God can deliver.

Jesus concludes this prayer saying, "If you forgive men
when they sin against you, then your heavenly Father will
forgive you, but if you do not forgive men their sins, your
heavenly Father will not forgive you." He made a condition
on the human desire for forgiveness. He said, "Your

forgiveness is limited by your willingness to forgive."

It is necessary for all believers to have forgiveness from God. It is very important that one ask for forgiveness in prayer. It is equally important for the believer to be willing to forgive people who have sinned against him or her. The Lord taught us that our prayer for forgiveness is conditioned on our willingness to forgive.

Jesus taught a great lesson on worship in the verses we have studied. It is important that believers worship, but it is imperative to worship correctly. Any act of worship that is done for personal physical gain is wasted.

Giving and praying for public display is hypocritical and wasted effort. Giving and praying for fellowship and obedience to God puts one in communication with God. This is worship at its best. The rewards of hypocritical worship are obvious. One wants to be seen and he is. That is all of the reward he gets. If one worships correctly, he has fellowship with God and receives the gifts God wants to give. Correct worship brings the best from God to the believer.

CHAPTER VI

THE TREASURES OF GOD

Matthew 6:16-34

It is very important for Christians to worship God. The praises that Christians bring to the Lord are important to Him. Each act of worship is significant. The passage of scripture under consideration in this chapter is a continuation of the passage studied in the last chapter. In the last chapter we saw the significance of giving and praying as worship. In this passage fasting is presented as an act of worship. Fasting was not to be done in order to be seen by people, but it was to be done as worship bringing the believer into communication with God. Jesus also taught in this passage that believers should treasure the presence of God. We have seen that Christians should call on the heavenly Father for things that they need, and He will answer those prayers.

I. The Treasure of Fasting

Fasting was and is a very important religious activity. When a believer fasts, he puts his entire attention on God. This causes him to turn from the ordinary things of human life. When the human life is lived in the power of God's Spirit, fasting becomes a necessity. Fasting is sometimes defined as not eating food. Fasting is not dieting or leaving off food for weight loss. It is not something that is done publicly in order to get God to do certain things.

Jesus talked about fasting as an act between a believer and God the heavenly Father.

There were people in Jesus' day that apparently fasted for public display. They evidently tousled their hair, contorted their faces, and went out in public so they would be seen. They hoped someone would say to them, "What is wrong with you?" That person would answer, "I am fasting." They wanted attention. Jesus said, "When you fast, fix your hair, using oil on your hair." They used olive oil. Jesus was saying, "Look nice." He told them to wash their faces. He wanted them to look as nice as they could. Their fasting was between them and God and was not to attract the attention of people.

What does this mean to believers today? Christians know that God is the source of all power. It is easy for one's attention to be captured by the world. When that happens one cannot maintain fellowship with God. Therefore, believers need to get their attention off the things of the world, and get their attention on the Lord. This might mean that one should do without food. It could require abstinence from other things. One must place God before physical things.

Fasting is an act of worship. Because it is, one does not boast about practicing it. One does not brag, saying, "I am fasting." One does not seek sympathy because they are depriving themselves of the ordinary. Instead the person who fasts places focus upon the Lord. When one fasts, prayers are intensified. The power of prayer becomes much greater.

Fasting increases fellowship with God and the intensity of fellowship with God becomes greater.

In the days of the Old Testament and New Testament, people fasted by not eating for a period of time. Jesus fasted for forty days. He apparently knew of the impending encounter with Satan and wanted to be spiritually prepared. That fast prepared His spirit for the need that existed. When Satan came, Jesus was able to resist all temptation.

Believers are blessed today by fasting. It is not to be done publicly. When a believer fasts, it is an act of worship between that person and God. In my life, I have fasted at times when I needed to move very close to the Lord. It has always been a great blessing. It has never been something to tell in public.

When one fasts as an act of worship the heavenly Father sees what is done in secret. He rewards openly. Prayer power and spiritual power are increased when attention is focused on God. This is not done for public attention, but for the love of God.

II. Heavenly Treasure

Jesus taught that service to God brings happiness. Service to God is related to what one treasures. The best treasures are in the Lord, not in physical things. Jesus said, "Do not store up for yourself treasures on earth where moth and rust destroy and where thieves break through and steal, but store up for yourself treasures in heaven, where moth and rust do not destroy and thieves do not break through and steal. For where your treasure is there will your heart be also."

To truly possess happiness requires an understanding of real treasures. Jesus said, "Where your treasure is there will your heart be also." One sets his heart on the thing that he loves most. Many people treasure their physical wealth above all else. They believe that if they have plenty of money and are affluent they have the blessings of God. They believe money is the most powerful thing in the world.

The Lord disagreed with that concept. He said, "Don't treasure earthly things; because they can be destroyed." One should not treasure what a moth can eat, such as clothes. Do not treasure what rust can consume, such as houses and cars. Trust in those things will bring great disappointment. Jesus taught Christians to lay up treasures in heaven. No one can take away those treasures.

What are heavenly treasures? All heavenly treasures are given by the grace of God. They come from Jesus Christ. The greatest treasure is salvation which comes to those who repent and have faith in Christ. He gives eternal life. One can treasure that. As one glories in that life, he will need to focus attention on the Lord who gave it. That results in service to God, which brings great reward. That service is motivated by love for God, and it brings eternal reward. One should treasure that service. He should also treasure the teaching of the word of God, because it is eternal. It will never pass away. It has meaning on earth, and it will have meaning in heaven. One should also treasure every experience of worship. The worship of God will not end when physical life ends. Christians will be in the presence of God for eternity. Worship will continue forever.

If one treasures the right things, he has eternal treasure that cannot be taken away. If one consumes life, seeking human glory and human possessions, he will fail. Many people fret through life, trying to hold their earthly treasures. If those treasures are not lost in life, they will be lost in death. When death comes, physical possessions have no significance. Heavenly treasures have eternal significance. They are far more important than earthly treasures.

III. No Double Standards

One who treasures heavenly things must be in control of his standards. He cannot have double standards. If one claims to be committed to the Lord, he cannot continue to treasure earthly things. The claim to love both is impossible. Jesus said, "The eye is the lamp of the body. If your eyes are good, your whole body will be full of light, but if your eyes are bad then your whole body will be full of darkness. If then the light within you is darkness, how great is that darkness."

Jesus taught that one could either see light with his eyes, or he was blind. He said that a blind person could not see light. He was referring to total blindness. If one is totally blind, he lives in darkness. One is either blind or he can see. Jesus meant that one who has spiritual sight treasures heavenly things. One cannot be blind and see. One cannot treasure the things of God and the things of the world. To make this matter clear the Lord gave another illustration. He said, "No one can serve two masters. Either he will hate the one or he will love the other, or else he will be devoted to the one and despise the other. You cannot serve God and money." One cannot be a slave to two masters. Both masters will require his services, and he will serve one or the other. God did not want part-time service. One's life cannot belong to God part-time.

God is talking about slavery. It is no accident that Paul repeatedly referred to himself as the slave or the bond servant of the Lord. He recognized that Christ was his Savior. He also acknowledged that Christ was his Lord. Because Jesus was his Lord, Paul referred to himself as one who was in the service of God. Each one saved by the grace of God is in the service of God and is in that sense the slave of the Lord. The Lord's illustration is a very appropriate one. If one tries to serve the world with his greatest ambition being to receive money, build houses, own cars, have bank accounts, or other worldly things, he will not serve God. The treasure must be in the Lord.

Which "master" will you serve? You must decide which one. If Jesus is your Savior and Lord, happiness can be secured in total service to Him. The only way one can be happy in this life and for eternity is to have the treasure of the Lord Jesus Christ in his heart.

IV. Treasured Promises

Jesus gave promises based on Christians' commitments to
Him. He said, "Therefore, I tell you do not worry about your
life, what you shall eat, or what you shall drink, or about
your body, what you will wear. Is not life more important
than food and the body more important than clothes. Look at
the birds of the air, they do not sow or reap or store away
in barns, and yet, your heavenly Father feeds them."

It is appropriate for God's children to serve Him in the
world. God promised to provide for all physical needs for
those who follow Him. One should never worry about this.
Yet, many fret continuously indicating their lack of trust in
God. God often told His followers not to be anxious, but to
live by faith. God knows that the human life is more
important than its appearance. The body which houses the
Spirit of God is more important than clothes.

God illustrated that the spiritual life is more
important than physical existence, and He will take care of
His people. He said, "Look at the birds, they do not do
anything in preparation to take care of their lives. They do
not sow; they do not reap, and they do not store in barns."
God created the birds and He takes care of them. God
provides the food for their sustenance. He provides a place
for the birds to nest. God gives the birds feathers. God
takes care of them in every way. He said, "Is not your life
more important than the birds." Not one bird falls out of the

air without the recognition of God. People are more important to God, so he will take care of them.

To be happy one must cease worrying about physical things. Do not worry about clothes, food, drink, houses, and cars. Have faith in the Lord. God will take care of all real needs. Believers must learn to be satisfied with God's gifts. If one is not satisfied with God's gifts, he either does not know God or he is out of fellowship with God. To know God, one must have knowledge of Jesus Christ. That is the way that God reveals Himself. One must receive Jesus Christ as Savior and Lord. When that is done the believer is brought into a right relationship with God. That relationship with God leads to fellowship with God. That fellowship can be broken by sins. The relationship is not lost, but the fellowship is broken. If one is more concerned with physical things then spiritual things, it may indicate that fellowship with God is broken. To get that right requires repentance and confession of sin. This brings the believer back into fellowship with God. That causes one to be satisfied with the wonderful gifts of God. God's gifts are better than physical things. Physical things do not last, but spiritual things are eternal. God said, "You are more valuable than any bird or anything."

Jesus said, "Remember this: By worrying you cannot add one hour to your life. You cannot add one cubit to your life." One cannot make himself taller by worrying. He cannot make himself shorter by anxiety. One cannot make himself more attractive or make his life last one hour longer by human worry. Jesus asked, "Why do you worry about clothes. See how the lilies of the field grow; they do not labor or spin yet I tell you that even Solomon in all of his splendor was not dressed like one of these. If that is how God clothes the grass of the field, which is here today and tomorrow is thrown into the fire, will God not much more take care of you; Oh, you of little faith."

Physical appearance is not as important as most people think. God wants His followers to think about more important things. He wants believers to consider eternal matters. He is capable of making human appearance very attractive. He made the beauty of the lily. A lily is beautiful whether one glances at it or scrutinizes it closely. The details of the lily are beautiful. Its leaves are attractive and its blossoms have a beautiful design. It was intricately designed by the power of God.

A lily dies and comes back to life from its roots the next year, resurrected into a new flower. It is again beautiful. How can this happen? God causes it to happen. God is saying, "If I can dress up the lilies like that, don't you think that I can make your life what it ought to be." God is talking about much more than physical things.

I know people who think that they are unimportant and they cannot accomplish anything. They feel defeated. God is saying, "Don't be like that. Don't go through life with a negative attitude worrying about what you can do or what you cannot do." Remember the one who made the beauty of the lily is the one who made you and who is taking care of you. He is going to make your life useful, if you will submit it to Him.

Jesus said, "Do not worry, saying, 'what shall we eat, or what shall we drink, or what shall we wear.' The pagans run after all these things, and my heavenly Father knows that you need them." God cares about all human needs. Believers are not to be as pagans who do not know God. Christians must trust God to take care of their physical and spiritual needs. God cares about each person and every need that exists. One can trust the Lord and He will provide.

God concludes this matter with a command. He said, "Seek first His kingdom and His righteousness and all these things will be given to you as well; therefore, do not worry about tomorrow for tomorrow will worry about itself. Each day has enough trouble of its own."

If one is a worrier and thinks only about physical things, every day will be full of trouble. If one thinks today is bad, tomorrow will be worse. That is the way life without God is. That is a terrible thing, but God does not want His children to live that way. One should seek first, the kingdom and the goodness of God. This should be the theme of life. The first thing every believer should want is the presence and the power of God. Every believer should seek the will of God. This would exclude living only for physical satisfaction. Commitment to God must be primary. When one does this, God makes a wonderful promise. He says,

"I will add all these things to you." God promised to add every physical need to the human life, if one places God and His kingdom first in life.

This is the way to be happy. People are not happy with physical things alone. They worry about them. Give yourself to God and God will give you spiritual things. Those spiritual things will take care of each need that you have in your life. God will also add His provisions for your physical needs.

I would rather have the presence and the power of God than anything else. I would rather have the answer to my prayers than the wealth of the world. I would rather know that I am walking in fellowship with God than anything else in this world.

CHAPTER VII
PRACTICAL ADVICE FOR HAPPINESS
Matthew 7:1-12

In the last chapter, Jesus taught that believers should seek His kingdom before all other things in life. In this chapter, He gives some practical advice on how to do that. When Jesus told His followers to seek first the kingdom of heaven, he advised them not to worry about the events of the day; because today can take care of itself. There is enough evil in the world today that we should not set our minds on tomorrow. We should concentrate on the power and the strength of the Lord for this hour.

It is in that context that Jesus gave the passage that we study in this chapter. There are three important concepts in this passage. First, Jesus talked about how to have the right relationship with other people by concentrating on one's own spiritual needs. He talked about how believers should be persistent in prayer. They should talk to the Lord and seek strength and power from the Lord. He then discussed other ethical relationships by giving the golden rule.

I. Victorious Ethics

Jesus said, "Do not judge or you will be judged. For in the same way that you judged others, you will be judged. And with the measure you use, it will be measured to you." There are many people who seem to think that criticizing other people is very entertaining. Many people waste a lot of time judging other people. The Lord plainly said, "Do not judge."

The Lord taught us several important things in this matter. He taught us that we must face the judgment of other people. The judgment that we face from other people will largely be determined by the attitude we have toward them. The standard a believer uses to measure others will be used by the one who judges him.

It is easy for some people to be critical of other people's wrongs. This is especially true if they do not have the same wrongs in their lives. Some people think that a sin is a terrible thing if they do not practice that particular sin. However, those same people are willing to overlook their own sins as insignificant. The Lord told His followers not to have that attitude. All people receive life from God; therefore, that life should be respected. That respect eliminates human judgment. If one is tempted to judge another, he should first try to understand the circumstances of the other person's life. That would eliminate most judgment.

Jesus taught His followers not to judge. Jesus said, "Why do you look at the speck of sawdust in your brother's eye and pay no attention to the plank in your own eye." Jesus used a figure of speech to explain the futility of judging others. Judging another person is like a sinner who is blinded by a large piece of wood in his eye trying to get a little speck out of another person's eye. He could not see to remove a speck from his brother's eye.

It is not fitting for a believer to criticize other people's lives while he does worse things in his life. Often people attempt to conceal their own sins by criticizing other people. Jesus taught that one should first rid himself of his own sins before he criticizes the sins of others. This attitude of criticism will keep a person from living for the glory of God and placing the kingdom of God and His righteousness first in his life.

Jesus addressed those who criticized others as "hypocrites." A hypocrite is one who is playing the game of religion. He does not really know the Lord. If a person spends his life being critical of other people, judging other people, speaking falsely of other people; he is acting hypocritically. This indicates that he is really playing the game of religion. He does not have things right in his heart with God.

When Jesus said, "Get the plank out of your eye," He was telling people to be certain about their own forgiveness before God. All sins need to be confessed to the Lord. After confession, sins must be left with the Lord, and there must be trust that He will forgive. The sinner must be cleansed by the blood of Jesus. His sacrifice is the atoning work for sin. One can get his life right by bringing his sins to Jesus in confession and faith. Then God makes the forgiven sinner useful. There is nothing more useless than a pretending Christian who criticizes other people, acting in self-righteousness and judgment.

Jesus concluded this matter by saying, "Do not give dogs what is sacred. Do not throw your pearls to pigs." In the religion of the Jews, dogs and pigs were unholy. People did not go near dogs and pigs. Both animals were considered "unclean." Jesus did not want His followers to waste their holy lives on unclean living. The human life is holy. God takes sin away and sanctifies human lives by forgiveness through the shed blood of His Son Jesus Christ. One's whole life becomes a holy thing that is in the hands of God. That life should not be wasted on unholy things. That holy life must not be thrown away in the world. Wasting the holy life is like throwing pearls in a pig pen. That would be throwing away a great treasure. Jesus also taught that the pigs would not appreciate pearls, but they might attack and hurt the one who had thrown the pearls. The holy life is not to be wasted in the sin of judgment. That makes holiness vulnerable to an attack from the world. Jesus taught that if people waste holy lives on criticism and judgment, which is worldly, the world will destroy those people and their holy lives.

One may be a believer in Christ, but he may be so out of fellowship with Him that he becomes critical of other people. That person is always looking for what is wrong in other people's lives. When one does that, he is wasting a holy life. One should not judge and criticize. He should see the value of all people as creatures of God. God placed each one in the world for His purpose. Believers should be helpful, not judgmental. That is the Lord's desire for all believers.

II. Persistence in Prayer

Obedience requires fellowship with God. Living in the presence of the Lord demands persistence in prayer. Jesus talked about that. He said, "Ask and it will be given you; seek and you will find; knock and the door will be opened unto you." These commands make wonderful promises. For these promises to be fulfilled requires believers to continuously ask, seek, and knock. God is talking about persistent prayer. One must have more than a formal prayer time. There needs to be more than a scheduled prayer time. When there is a need, believers should ask God. When there is an opportunity, believers should knock. Believers should always stay before the Lord and continuously seek the face of the Lord.

God has made many wonderful promises in the Bible about prayer. It is strange that He must continuously tell us that we should pray. People spend little time praying. God wants us to ask all the time, seek all the time, and knock all the time. Ask, seek, and knock are related concepts. One must ask God for his needs. He must seek the face of God. He also is to knock on the door of opportunity which is the presence of God. The one who asks, receives. Everyone who seeks, finds. All who knock, have the door opened to them.

Sometimes people appear to seek but do not find. What is the reason for this? It is possible for people to pray improperly. Sometimes people pray selfishly. James said, "When you ask you do not receive because you ask with wrong motives, that you may spend what you get on your pleasures" (Ja. 4:3). When people pray selfishly, God is not interested in their prayers. Those prayers are not answered. That is not seeking. Sometimes people pray outside of the will of the Lord. That is not seeking. One must discover the will of God, then live in the will of God. Prayer can be made in the will of God, and God will hear and answer. When believers meet God's conditions, God promises that He will hear and He will answer. It is wonderful to know that a believer can ask and God will give. One should determine that all prayer will be made in the will of the Lord and for the glory of the Lord rather than for human glory. God will answer those prayers.

Jesus promised that if one seeks he will find. What is he to seek? In prayer one must seek the face of God. This means that he seeks the presence of God. When one seeks the face of God, his own pride and lusts are eliminated, causing him to give all his life to the purpose of God.

To knock means to search for opportunities in the will of God. God will show His will and open the door of opportunity to those who persistently come to the Lord. It is sensible to believe that God gives to His children who ask of Him. Jesus said, "Which of you, if his son asks for bread will give him a stone or if he asks for fish will give him a snake?" Parents understand this. When a child needs something and asks for it, the parent gives it if it is possible. When that child says, "I am hungry. I need a

piece of bread," the parent does not give the child a stone
to eat. The parent gives bread. If the child needs meat,
the parent gives meat, not a snake. The parent gives the
child what is proper and good. The parent gives what is best
for the child. All good parents do that. So, Jesus said,
"If we know how to give good gifts as sinful people, how much
more will your Father in heaven give good gifts to those who
ask Him." The question here, "How much more," is of great
significance. If humans take care of their own, how much
more will our heavenly Father take care of His own? The
answer to that requires one to examine the quality of God's
love. Human love is never perfect; God's love is always
perfect. His love is the greatest love in the world. The
love of the heavenly Father has been consistent since the
beginning of time. When Adam and Eve sinned, immediately the
heavenly Father provided a way for forgiveness and escape;
because He loved them. Every generation since then has
experienced the love of God. Even when the people rebelled
against God's love and broke His law, God loved and forgave
them. In the days of Jeremiah when the people strayed far
from the Lord, God's hand of judgment came down upon them.
However, Jeremiah, the preacher of God, told about the love
of God. He told them that God was willing to forgive and
bring them back.

In the eighth century before Christ, when the people
were in the ways of the world, and had turned from God, He
continued to send His prophets one after another to say,

"Turn to me; I love you; I will forgive you." The people were worshipping idols. They were following Baal, but God continued to promise forgiveness if they would repent and return to Him. In the New Testament era God sent His Son to establish forgiveness for His people. Jesus came as the final and ultimate expression of the love of God. Jesus the Son of God humbled Himself and became a servant and was obedient unto death. He died the terrible death on the cross (Phil. 2:5-10). This tells us about the greatness of the love of God. God by His power raised Jesus from the dead. God sent the Holy Spirit to call us to faith and to minister to our lives. All of this is telling us, "How much more the heavenly Father loves us."

I have been loved in life by my wife, my parents, my children, and my grandchildren. I am loved by them and by many of my friends, but I know that there is no greater love than the love of God. The heavenly Father loves us more than all others. Because He does, He will answer our prayers. We know that He will give us the things that we need, and He will take care of us. He knows how to give good gifts to His people. Believers sometimes ask for things that they do not need. God will not give that. He gives good gifts. He gives the gifts that are needed.

Let us go through life seeking first the kingdom of God and His righteousness. Do not judge others. Talk to the Lord, asking for the things that you need and He will provide those things.

III. The Golden Rule

Jesus concluded this by saying, "So, in everything do unto others what you would have them do to you; for this sums up the law and the prophets." We call this the golden rule. This rule appears in many other religions. Our Lord said whatever you want people to do to you, you do to them. Then He said that this is the summary of the law and prophets. Everything God taught in the law and everything God taught in the prophets can be summarized in obedience to this command. God taught His followers to respect all people. All people have relationships to other people. Each person should respect all other people. God made all people, so all are of value to Him and should be of value to each other.

God wants all people to treat other people the same way they want to be treated. How do you want God to treat you? You want God to treat you as the recipient of love and provide for you by His grace all the things that you need. Therefore, since you know the Lord, you should treat other people the way you want God to treat you. How do you want other people to treat you? You want to be treated with respect. You do not want someone to be bigoted against you. You do not want someone to judge you, but you want to be respected. You want to be honored when honor is due. You want openness and love. God says if that is what you want from other people, then give that to other people. Usually when one gives that kind of respect to other people, his lif commands respect from other people.

78

It is interesting what a smile can do. When someone is speaking evil toward you, smile and show love in that smile. Evil could disappear. God taught that He built the whole principle of Christianity on the golden rule. It is the summary of all the law and the prophets. If one desires to obey the law and the prophets, he must treat other people the way he wants to be treated. That can be done in the strength of the Lord. That is the way God operates. People need to be sure that they know Jesus Christ. He must be in charge of all the actions of the lives of those people. God will help you to treat other people the way you want to be treated. Happiness requires an understanding of one's relationship to God and His relationship to other people. Believers should not judge other people, they should love and understand other people as God's creation. In order to be successful in having the love of God and demonstrating the love of God, one needs to learn to depend upon the Lord. That dependence upon the Lord requires persistence in prayer. One should ask God for everything he needs. He needs to ask God for victory over criticism and judgment.

One needs to seek the face of God. He also needs to knock on the door of opportunity that he might do what God wants done. In order to practice good relationships with other people, the golden rule needs to be applied to the human life. God taught that we should respect each other as God's created people. To do this, we must walk with the Lord in total surrender to Him as the Master of our lives.

CHAPTER VIII

FACING PERILS TO HAPPINESS

Matthew 7:13-28

People that recognize Jesus as the Lord know that the
"Sermon on the Mount" is very significant. Jesus taught
believers how to properly relate to other people and how to
walk with God. He taught believers to pray and worship. In
the concluding paragraph of the "Sermon on the Mount" Jesus
told believers about the many perils they would have to face
as God's people because the world is filled with sin. Jesus
is the solid foundation on which believers must build their
lives.

There are many perils that face Christians in their
journey through life. When Christians face those perils,
they need to place complete trust in the Lord as the Solid
Rock. Jesus called the wide gate and the flat road a peril.
This was understood by His followers because they knew about
the various roads and gates that were entrances to Jerusalem.
On holy days, great crowds of people came to Jerusalem.
There were wide gates and narrow gates that offered entrance
to the city. At a wide gate, large crowds could enter the
city. The road at that gate was flat, making it easy to
enter the city. There were many narrow gates--like the
Eastern gate. To enter by the Eastern gate one must ascend a
hill and enter through a narrow gate. It is much more
difficult to enter the city through these gates.

I. The Perils Enumerated

The Lord implied that people tend to search for the broad gates and the flat roads. The Lord taught that some people searched for the easiest way in their religion. People who search for the easy way are doing what the majority does. They find what is popular and follow that path. That is a great peril. Many people confess faith in Jesus Christ and serve God for awhile, then they go back into the ways of the world. Some claim to have great faith in the Lord, yet, in a short time, they go back to doing the things they did when they did not know the Lord. These people have fallen into the peril of the wide gate and the flat road.

The Lord said that there is a narrow gate and a narrow road. Believers should walk through the narrow gate. Jesus said, "Small is the gate and narrow is the road that leads to life and only a few find it." The wide gate leads to destruction; but the narrow gate leads to life. The Lord taught that human lives are wasted if they are not lived in the way of the Lord. The way of the world is opposite of the way of the Lord. The world's way brings one to destruction. If one only lives for human pleasure life is wasted. However, many people, perhaps most people, live on the broad road of human pleasure. Many people are very reluctant to do what God wants because that is not what the majority of people are doing. The way that is followed by the majority leads to destruction.

The narrow gate and narrow road symbolize the way God wants believers to live. One should find what God wants done and do it. That will lead to an abundant life (Jn. 10:10). In order to have an abundant life, one must walk on the narrow road with the Lord. One must discover what the will of God is and do what God tells him to do. How do you do this? Believe God's word. Stay in the word and discover what the word teaches, then do what the word of God says. One must stay in fellowship with God through prayer and commitment to Him as the Lord. To stay in this narrow way, one must also have fellowship with other believers who walk in the narrow way. Sometimes Christians who serve the Lord are called "fanatics." Remember the way is narrow and may appear to be fanatical. Followers of Jesus must walk with the Lord and not walk in the ways of the world. The invitation to worldliness is a constant peril to believers. Faithful service to Jesus as Lord is its antidote.

Jesus called false prophets a dangerous peril. He said that false prophets would say they came from God. The world invites the children of God to turn away from the Lord and follow its ways. Some people who call themselves prophets of God will say, "Follow me." Jesus warned that believers should beware of false prophets. He said that they will come in sheep's clothing, but inwardly they are hungry wolves. They can be identified by the fruit they produce. They will pretend to be religious or even religious leaders. God says do not believe false prophets, disguised as sheep, pretending to be teachers and saints of God. These prophets will invite people to follow them, but do not be deceived because they are really hungry wolves who desire power over other people.

The people who first heard the "Sermon on the Mount," were shepherds or they knew about the work of shepherds. They knew that the intention of a wolf was always to devour the sheep. Jesus warned that some humans were like wolves. Their one intention was to capture people for their own benefit. Jesus taught that false prophets do not have a benevolent interest in other people. The fact that they wore sheep's clothes meant that they would say that they had a concern for peoples needs, but they had no real interest in anyone but themselves. False prophets want to use the lives of other people for their own benefit because they are hungry wolves. False prophets are a peril to be avoided.

Sometimes this peril is difficult to avoid. Believers are inclined to believe in people who say that they are sent from God. Jesus taught that the fruit of the prophet's labors should be examined. Jesus said, "Do people pick grapes from thorn bushes or figs from thistles, likewise, every good tree bears good fruit and every bad tree bears bad fruit. A good tree cannot bear bad fruit and a bad tree cannot bear good fruit."

Some of the audience of the "Sermon on the Mount" were shepherds and some were farmers. The farmers raised grapes. Jesus said, "When you go out to pick grapes, you don't go to a thorn tree, you go to a grapevine to pick grapes." Jesus taught that the life of the person who says, "I am a religious person," should bear good fruit. What is the fruit that should be born by believers in Christ? One should practice the faith that one preaches. The practice of that faith bears a constant witness that will cause other people to come to know Christ.

What kind of fruit are you bearing? Are you bearing fruit that would cause people to see the working of God in your life? Can people really see that you are saved by the grace of God? This is the fruit that should be seen. If other people are not coming to know Jesus Christ because of the fruit of your life, then you need to make sure about your relationship with the Lord. Believers also need to make sure that they walk with the Lord every day.

Jesus taught that a good tree cannot bear bad fruit. If a prophet is truly sent from God, he teaches the word of God and lives by the word of God. He will not bear bad fruit, because he cannot. God brings success to the true prophet. The word of God is, "Quick and powerful and sharper than any two edged sword." The word of God must be delivered by a clean vessel. That kind of prophet will bear good fruit because he is sent from God.

Jesus said that the false prophet will be judged. He said, "Every tree that does not bear good fruit is cut down and thrown into the fire, thus by their fruit you will recognize them." Believers need to understand that God will deal with false prophets. They will be cut down and thrown into the fire. God will bring their efforts to nothing. They will have to face God and account for their works in judgment. Jesus said, "Not everyone who says to me, Lord, Lord, will enter into the kingdom of heaven."

Another peril is the possibility of false confessions. Many people say, "Jesus is my Lord; I follow Jesus." They call Him Lord, but they do not do the will of the Father. When one does not do the will of the Father, he is not following Jesus as Lord. Following Jesus as Lord is more than talking, it is doing something. When one commits his life to Jesus in faith, Jesus is recognized as Savior and Lord of that life. He cannot be Savior without being Lord. For Him to be the Lord requires commitment to the will of the Father. Conversion to Him as Lord involves both saying and doing. The Bible says, "With the heart a man believes unto righteousness and with the mouth confession is made unto salvation." Confession must come from the heart though it is spoken from the mouth. If one believes in his heart that Jesus is Savior and Lord he wants to do what God tells Him to do. Jesus said, "Not everyone who says to me Lord, Lord will enter into the kingdom of heaven but only he who does the will of my Father who is in heaven." Some people make confession of their sins, but do nothing to change. When one receives Jesus as Savior, he should be obedient to openly confess Him as Lord. The believer must declare to the world that he is the child of God. In a confession of faith, one must unite with the other children of God and spread the word of the Lord around the world. Jesus said to His disciples, "You shall be witnesses unto me wherever you are" (Acts 1:8). This is the will of the Father. It is the will of the Father that we live the way God teaches us to live in His word. It is God's will for believers to become obedient servants. Jesus said, "You are my friends if you do whatever I have commanded you." To express your friendship with Him as the Lord of your life demands obedience to Him in all things.

Jesus said, "Many will say unto me in that day, Lord, Lord, did we not prophesy in your name and in your name drive out demons and perform miracles, then I will tell them plainly, I never knew you, go away from me evildoers." Jesus knew that there were people who were making false confessions. He also knew that some would go to the day of judgment making false confessions. They think that because they did work in His name, cast out demons, prophesied and did miraculous things they will be all right with God. The Lord will answer, "You did not do it by my power; I do not know you. Depart from me." What a terrible day that is going to be for people who try to be saved by their works.

The Bible says that it is not by works of righteousness that we have done but according to His mercy. He has saved us by the washing, regeneration and the renewing of the Holy Ghost" (Tit. 2:5). God does the saving by His own power. The saved are then to live with God while living on earth. When their lives here on earth are finished, they will be taken to heaven to live with the Lord forever. Instead of hearing the tragic words, "Depart from me I never knew you," the children of God will be with the Lord. Make sure that you really know Jesus as Savior. You should be expressing that saved life by recognizing Jesus as the Lord of your life.

II. The Solid Rock of Safety in the Time of Peril

The Lord concludes the "Sermon on the Mount" by saying that everyone who hears these words and does them is like a person who builds his house on a solid foundation. He said, "The one who hears these words and does not practice them is like one who builds his house on the sand." The person who builds his house on the sand is in grave danger. When the wind, rain, and floods continue beating upon the foundation of that house, it will fall. The winds, rains, and floods symbolize the cares of the world. Cares of the world can be like a storm beating at your life. Finally, the human life will succumb to those cares and will fall.

Jesus said, "There is a solid rock." It has a foundation. That rock is Jesus. When Jesus was still on earth, He asked His disciples if they knew who He was. Simon Peter said, "You are the Christ, the Son of the Living God." Jesus replied, "Blessed are you, Simon, son of Jonah, for this was not revealed to you by men, but by my Father in heaven, and I tell you that you are Peter and upon this rock I will build my church and the gates of hell will not overcome it" (Matt. 16:16-18). Jesus named Simon a rock because he understood that Jesus was the Christ - the Son of the Living God. Jesus then said, "Upon this rock I will build my church." The word He used for Simon was "<u>Petros</u>." He said He would build His church upon the "<u>Petra</u>." The rock upon which the church was built is the rock of Jesus Christ. Because Jesus is the Christ, the Son of the Living God, the church is built upon Him. Peter later referred to Jesus as the Living Stone. He said, "As you come to Him, the Living Stone, rejected by men but chosen by God and precious to Him, you also, like living stones, are being built into a spiritual house to be a holy priesthood offering spiritual sacrifices acceptable to God through Jesus Christ, for in the scripture it says, 'See, I lay a stone in Zion, a chosen and precious cornerstone, and the ones who trust in Him will never be put to shame'" (I Pet. 2:4-6). Peter understood that the rock of our salvation is Jesus Christ. He is a solid foundation. Anyone who builds his life on the person of Jesus has a secure life. From Jesus Christ believers receive eternal life--life that will never be taken away.

God said, "Put your life in Jesus Christ. Let Him be the foundation of your life." How do you do that? Receive Him as the Son of God and as your Savior. Receive Him to be your personal Savior and Lord by faith. Believe that He is the one who died for you and the one who is raised from the dead. Believe that he is the one who can give you eternal life, and that He is the one who can guide and protect your life now. You put your life on the solid foundation by putting your life in Jesus Christ. On that solid foundation you are able to stand in difficult times. The threatening perils of life will be unable to remove you from the solid foundation of Jesus Christ.

The Lord said many wonderful things in the "Sermon on the Mount." In the conclusion to that great sermon the Lord told us that we would find real happiness if we would submit ourselves to Him and let Jesus be our Savior and Lord. The solid foundation of Jesus Christ will make it possible for us to do the things that He taught in the "Sermon on the Mount." The result will be real happiness.